The Eight Principles to Inner Peace

A Spiritual Guidebook
To A Joyous, Free & Abundant Life

Teachings of the Light Collective

Dorothy Lee
Author

Kathryn Harwig
Channel

INSIGHT
A Wyatt-MacKenzie Imprint

The Eight Principles to Inner Peace
A Spiritual Guidebook To A Joyous, Free & Abundant Life
Teachings of the Light Collective

by Dorothy Lee, Author, and Kathryn Harwig, Channel

ISBN: 978-0-9743832-7-9

Published by INSIGHT, A Wyatt-MacKenzie Imprint

INSIGHT
A Wyatt-MacKenzie Imprint

For Imprint information visit: www.WyMacPublishing.com

Requests for permission or further information should be addressed to:
Wyatt-MacKenzie Publishing, 15115 Highway 36,
Deadwood, Oregon 97430

Acknowledgments

I would like to say "thank you," and send a big hug to Barbara Wolfe, Constance Hope, Patricia Johnson, and my granddaughter Victoria Schwartz for their encouragement, inspiration, and assistance with writing this book And a special thank you to Debra Davis for not only assisting with the writing of the book, but providing the beautiful cover photo of the rising sun.

To Kathryn Harwig and the Light Collective, a special thank you for agreeing to hold Light Collective Speaks sessions. Your extensive knowledge of the universe and humans can now be shared

Contents

INTRODUCTION
1

The Only Way We Will Obtain Peace Upon
The Planet
5

Many Lives, Many Beings, Many Dimensions
7

Only An Illusion
11

One Of The Most Powerful Things In The Cosmos
13

You Have A Choice
17

There Is No "Good" or "Bad"
21

You Are Greatly Admired & Feared By Other Beings
25

ABOUT THE CHANNEL
29

ABOUT THE AUTHOR
31

INTRODUCTION

This guidebook is based on the teachings of the Light Collective, a group of nonphysical beings channeled by Kathryn Harwig, internationally acclaimed psychic/medium, author, and speaker. The Light Collective has been communicating with humans for eons. Three years ago they asked Kathryn to channel at forums for the pubic because our current behavior is interfering with the cosmos. They state: *"We have spoken to your species for eons through numerous beings that were capable of interpreting for us, however, at this time in your history it has become important that you cease, or at least attempt to cease, some of your ways for it is being disruptive of other dimensions including ours."* The Eight Principles To Inner Peace is based on their teachings at these forums.

The Light Collective is a group of beings from another dimension. Because they have the ability to travel to many dimensions, aren't constrained by time or space, and can tune into multiple dimensions at one time, they have access to a great deal of information from the universe.

They recognize that our disruptive behavior is part of a process of great spiritual and social change, and in order to survive and thrive through that change, we are in need of the knowledge they can provide.

Their name, The Light Collective, is a descriptive name. They don't have bodies, and while they are individuals, they are also a collective and function as such. If we were to see them, we would see beautiful dancing light. They are telepathic, and explain that humans have the same ability but were systematically trained not to use it. For us to understand telepathy we need to understand on the deepest level, that we are all one. They say that in the near future, many of us will be able to use this ability, and this will be a great benefit to mankind.

The Light Collective is in the process of learning our language, so you may notice some unusual sentence structure, grammar, and "coined" words in some of their quotes.

The Light Collective's teachings are based on, in their words, "Principles for a joyous, free, and abundant life". They tell us the principles are not new knowledge; there is no new knowledge in the universe or the cosmos. Wise humans have been aware of the principles for as long as there have been humans on the planet, which is a very long time - much longer than we've been told by our history. According to the Light Collective, these principles are universal, and are followed by them as well as others in the cosmos.

The Light Collective says we are in a dark period of history, and, in their attempt to assist us in our journey through change and a new way of life, they say, *"Part of our goal is teaching you of your power. Human beings are one of the most powerful beings in a large and highly populated cosmos. You have been routinely and systematically told differently. Do not blame your parents or your husband, for that is part of the culture. Now it is time for you to learn the truth."* Four of their principles teach us how to use our power.

I am excited to share these principles with you. I learned of them at Kathryn's Light Collective Forums, and realized they are a foundation and guide for using spiritual wisdom in everyday life. The knowledge and strategies they provide have allowed me to create the life I desire, but more importantly, they have changed the way I feel. The Eight Principles have given me feelings of security, power, peace, and joy. I am confident that they will do the same for you!

May The Eight Principles bring you a joyous, free, & abundant life!

Love, Dorothy

The Divine Is The Sum Total Of All Beings
—The Light Collective

The Only Way We Will Obtain Peace Upon The Planet

Principle One
We Are All One

The first and most important principle is "all beings are one." Everything in the world is made of energy. All beings, animate and inanimate, seen and unseen, beings in other dimensions, all beings in the universe are made of energy. This energy is interconnected to a universal energy field, referred to as "the Force" in the Star Wars movies.

Energy is vibrations, so everything is also made up of vibrations. The Light Collective says they see us as a dancing pattern of light. They believe we would love the fact that we are all connected to each other and go deep in the earth, high into the sky, and extend in many, many directions with beautiful colors.

We all contribute to the creation of this energy field with the thoughts and emotions we send out, which, of course, are in the form of energy just as everything else in the universe is. And we are able to tap into this energy field to access the knowledge of the universe and communicate with each other.

The Light Collective says: *"You are all one with one another. If you believed that and knew that in the depth of your heart, it would be rather hard to kill each other. It is part of our goal to teach you that you are all one, for that is the only way that you will attain peace upon your planet."*

God, of course, is also connected to all beings. The Divinity, the Divine God is the collection of all beings. It is a loving collection. There is no fear in this Divinity. There is no reason for you to ever fear God, for God is a loving God, not a judgmental, condemning, punishing God.

God is a being in and of God self, of course, but God is also the sum total of all beings. The Divine has the knowledge of all beings. Anything that would happen to any one being in any one cosmos would be in the awareness of the Divine. When you pray to the Divine you are in fact answered always because the Divine is responding to itself. The Divine has provided enough of everything we need on earth to live in peace, harmony, and joy.

Heaven is a term created by one of our religions, and it is a term to define the return to the divinity. The term hell is when a spirit, for whatever reason, decides that they do not desire to return to the divine.

Your security will come in knowing
That the universe always supports you,
　　　　　　　—The Light Collective

Most of you would know in your heart
As you search it
That if you were eternal
You would therefore have to live somewhere;
This would make sense, would it not?
—The Light Collective

Many Lives, Many Beings, Many Dimensions

Principle Two

We Are Eternal

All major religions of the world believe in the concept of eternal life. Our life here on earth was not our beginning, and our death will not be an ending. The Light Collective explains it this way: *"There is no way for you not to exist. This is true of all beings. Since you are eternal, it's wise to spend eternity in a joyful state, and a growth state. Eternity is a long time and you must do something. Therefore you periodically decide to come to various places and be various people, and also various beings on other cosmos and other planets."*

"Many, if not all of you have lived lives on other planets, and certainly all of you have lived in other dimensions or spirit, the world you go to after you pass is another dimensional state. Heaven, as you call it, is another dimensional state, many other dimensional states."

"Your defining characteristic is your curiosity. You will not forget anything that you have learned on this planet nor any other time.

When you cease to become a human being and return to spirit you will analyze what you have learned and you will decide what you would further wish to learn. Perhaps you will return here for another bout of humanness, or perhaps you will return to another dimension or being in another place."

There are a multitude of dimensions, in a multi-layered world. In between your lives on this planet you may choose to go to other planets or other dimensions and become different entities.

When you ask the Light Collective what will happen in the future, they can predict based only on your personality as of that date, for you have total and complete control of your life.

As a human being we have four layers.

The first layer is our physical animal body, which deteriorates and eventually ceases to exist. It has a consciousness in and of itself. When we go from body to body we carry with us DNA, and it has memories from our ancestors, but it is a limited memory, and limited emotions reside in our animal body.

The second layer is our soul, our eternal being; the piece of us that always has been and always will be. The soul resides within our animal body, although it is free to leave and does frequently when we sleep or other times when our soul is capable of leaving the body. The soul is where our consciousness, our intention, and our decisions are made. This is also where we create most of our relationships. It is innate in all souls to grow, to learn, to change.

Within our soul we also have a personality. Many of us think this is who we are. This is the being that we give a name to, and who speaks to us. When we die and pass into spirit our personality is only one of many we have had. In spirit we live full lives, free of the challenges of earth, and we are able to visit and watch over our loved ones who are still here on earth.

The third layer is our soul collective. It's made up of many souls who have decided to join into being for the purpose of attaining their goals, largely to learn and grow. We came to earth because this is an optimum place to grow, and to be joyful under the circumstances we have chosen and created.

We don't retain our memories when we come to earth for two reasons. One is that we wish to learn new things with new memories. Also, coming to earth is considered to be a rather sensory experience, and sensory experiences are fresh when you have not experienced them before.

Your soul collective could be thousands or hundreds of thousands of beings, but not all beings. Part of your soul collective is not on this planet. Your guides are part of your soul collective who stayed in another dimension so that they can aid you by speaking to you and guiding you. Some of your soul collective are not human beings. Some are light beings, so the Light Collective might be part of your soul collective. There are many more beings than we can imagine on, in and off our planet.

The fourth layer is the entire collective all of beings, the ultimate of what you would call God, God being the total and sum complete of all the collectives and in contact with all beings in all dimensions. This takes us back to the first principle that We Are All One. The Light Collective says *"Your fourth level of beingness is one in which you can dance with God, or the stars, or the lake. Know at some point you are as much that part, as one drop of your blood is* a part of your body. While your blood may not be conscious of that, it is still entirely a part of a functioning human body."

The Light Collective concludes their explanation by saying *"And now we have discussed the four layers of your being, and that these layers are eternal. Your animal body will change into something quite different, and you will leave it. You will retain your personality once you pass on to spirit. You will remember being you. You will simply remember it in the context of all the yous that you have been, and all the yous that you will be, and all the yous that you could be. You are much greater, much larger, much more beautiful and much lighter than you may have thought that you were."*

Time is merely a
Measuring device
—The Light Collective

Only An Illusion

Principle Three
Time Is An Illusion

The Light Collective explains that time is an illusion, and merely a measuring device created by humans as a way of ordering our lives. It's not linear, but rather like a porous structure. There are a multitude of dimensions, making a multi-layered world. It's entirely possible to reincarnate into the future, or to reincarnate into the past. In between your lives on this planet you may choose to go to other planets or other dimensions and become different entities.

When you go back to spirit you are not just a personality, but you are all the selves that you have been, all the selves that you will be, and all the selves that you can be.

It is possible for you to go to the past and change it, and it is possible for you to go to the future and change that. If you ask the Light Collective what will happen, they can predict based only on your personality as of that date, for you have total and complete control, and you cannot only change your future, you can change your past.

While we are living here on earth, these concepts are difficult to grasp. But the Light Collective does give us the following practical advice concerning time: *"If you remember that time is an illusion, then you also remember that it is your tool, and if you desire you have control of your time. Your language dictates to you much of what you do. When you says things like "I am running out of time" or "I don't have time for this" or "time is going too fast" that makes it so. It would be wise for you, if you were feeling that way, to say "I have plenty of time" or "Time is of no meaning to me" or Whatever I need to do will be done in the time I wish to give it."*

The human species is a powerful species,
Not powerful with guns and killing,
But powerful with intention and joy.
—The Light Collective

One Of The Most Powerful Things In The Cosmos

Principles Four & Five

You Create With Your Thoughts
You Activate Your Thoughts With Your Emotions

The Light Collective explains: *"The next four principles are all related, as of course all of these principles are related. They dance lovely dances with each other, and the words waltz. The next four principles have to do with how you can live your lives and create joyous, free, and abundant lives."*

"You have amazing power. Your ability to control your emotions could be one of the most powerful things in the cosmos. Every one of you is capable of controlling your emotions, and you have been told you cannot. Because of this you have created a culture of victims. We have come here, as have many others, to tell you to claim your power of intention, and to claim your power of emotion."

As the Light Collective tells us above, our thoughts and our emotions are very powerful. We create our lives with them whether we are aware of this or not. We all can have joyous, free, and abundant lives if we claim our power of intention (thought) and our power of joy (emotion).

All things in your life are created in a two-step process. Step one—create with your intention, or your thoughts. In order to create exactly what you want, it is important to be specific. Make sure you state what you want, not what you don't want. That confuses the universe. A guide to deciding what you want is to ask, "What brings me joy, or what would bring me joy?"

Once you have stated clearly what you want, go to step two—activate those thoughts with your emotions. You can create, but unless you activate it is very similar to making a car but not putting fuel in it. You have a car, but the car has no motion, it can't work. Emotions are the fuel that activates your thoughts. It's important to keep your emotions love based because love is a natural emoter for the human species and is much more powerful than fear based emotions.

You don't have to be concerned with how you will receive what you desire. Allow the universe to do it for you. Remember, you are powerful—you create your world with your thoughts and emotions, the Divine has provided enough of everything you need, and the universe always supports you. Act and feel as though you have already received what you desire. Your love based emotions of trust and faith will assist in creating what you desire.

Action may be required on your part. Be alert to opportunities and actions you may need to take.

If the action is in line with what you desire, it will feel joyous and effortless.

Just as we create our world as individuals, we also create our world as soul collectives. We work with our soul collective to come up with a common plan that will enhance the growth of all in the collective. The current changes taking place on earth at this time are the result of soul collective action that began in 1968.

Your society is lying to you in saying
You must pay attention to this or that
Or the other thing that is fearful.
To be brave is to live in a joyful state.
—The Light Collective

You Have A Choice

Principle Six
There are Two Basic Emotions, Love & Fear

Many people believe we have many emotions, but all emotions are really either love based or fear based. The closer you can come to identifying your emotions as love or fear, the closer you are to determining which emotion is driving you.

Fear is a very powerful fuel, but love is a much more powerful emotion. If fifty people are love based, they can cancel five thousand negative fear based people. It is a much more powerful vibration level.

The first step to mastering emotions is to acknowledge that you are capable of doing so. Most of us have been taught that we are not in control of our emotions and so we say "this person has made me so angry," as opposed to "I choose to be angry because this person has said this." It's a minor but very important distinction. Realize that no one can force you, and no thing can force you to feel a fear based emotion.

How do you get over fear? First you acknowledge that it exists. Don't see it as something other than fear. When you say you are nervous or apprehensive, you are fearful. There are many fear emotions and they can highly motivate and drive your thought process, but usually with a large cost to you.

Many people are more comfortable being angry than they are of being fearful, and so they feel that anger has power. But anger is a fear emotion. When you use anger it's wise to say "I know that anger is a fear emotion, and I can choose to be fearful, but at least I can acknowledge that that is what it is."

Depression is a fear emotion – fear you have lost something, will lose something, or something will not return to you. Anxiety if also a fear emotion, however, in this case we often can't put a name to our specific fear.

It is always appropriate to label fear as fear because then you can decide whether it is suiting you or not. When you call fear anger, or when you call fear logic, then it is much harder to deal with.

Circumstances can elicit sadness. Sadness and emptiness never serve a higher purpose. All higher purposes are aided by love and joy. When you are feeling sad, first ask, "Is there anything I can do to change the circumstance? If not, is there a way I can feel joy and live in this position?"

When you are thinking in a fearful fashion you are still activating your thoughts, but probably in a way you don't desire. For example, let's say that you have decided that you will make a great deal of money and you are determined that that will be so. You have been raised to be afraid of being poor. You will say, "I'm afraid I will never have any money, and I must make money, therefore I'm going to think about making money because I'm so afraid that I won't have money". Your thought pattern is that "I will make money", but your emotional driving fuel behind it is fear. It is entirely possible that you will make money, but perhaps in the process you will destroy your health, or destroy your personal relationships, for you are creating what you desire, but you are creating it from a fear basis.

As a contrast you could think, "It would be wonderful to have money, for then I would have the ability to have a compassionate and joyful life, and I know I can create this because I am a powerful and wise being." Then you would feel calm and confident. This emotion would be a love based emotion, and would also create money for you, as much money as you needed.

No one can make you angry and no one can make you love him or her. No one can make you do anything. You are in total control of your own emotions. It's your destiny, because once you have chosen to claim that, you will never again feel that you are under manipulation. But until that time, you are being manipulated to feel fear at all times. For example, when you watch the media and they say this is happening and it will be horrible, and the earth is dying and it is being poisoned, you can say "I choose not to be afraid and I will act or I will not act, in any case, I don't need to feel fear just because they are telling me that I should do so." It won't change in any way shape or form, what is happening. Your emotions will only change yourself. But if you change, the soul collective changes, and then all beings change by the fact that you changed.

*Underneath anger and grief is fear, and underneath it all
is love and forgiveness.*
—The Light Collective

*You have a choice.
Your choice is to be free of fear.
Or your choice is to be haunted by fear.
It is time to release your selves from fear.*
—The Light Collective

Love is a more efficient tool.
Not because it is good,
Not because God wants you to love,
It is because it is efficient
And more likely to create what you have thought.
It is a scientific principle.
—The Light Collective

There Is No "Good" or "Bad"

Principle Seven
Choose Love

The most important thing about choosing love is the word "choose". You have control of your emotions. Every emotion is your choice. Every one.

The Light Collective says: *But then you will say to us "Light Collective, if I am seeing a car heading toward me, and I feel fear, is that a choice?" And we would say to you "Yes it is a choice after approximately one or two of your seconds." First you would feel a fear, and this would perhaps be an emotion of startleness, and you would not be able to think. You have all been in a situation where you cannot think. Fear will stop you from thinking. Of course you cannot create, you cannot think, but we assure you that in short order you will think, for you cannot not think. And when you do you have a choice of feeling a fear based emotion which would be "I am going to be hit by a car and I am so afraid" or a love based emotion which is "I am going to be hit by a car and I should get out of the way, and it would be good for me to do so."*

Even in that most extreme case you have a choice of acting out of fear, which would be "I will die now, I am afraid I will die." Or love, which is "I choose to be strong and make the best attempt to save myself." In either case it is not the car that is heading toward you that has caused this emotion, it is your choice. When you recognize and are willing to acknowledge that all within one second of every happening you are choosing your emotion.

Just as there are many fear based emotions, there are many love based emotions. Confidence, compassion, joy, eagerness, and playfulness, and many, many more are love based emotions. Sometimes it's not clear whether an emotion we are feeling is love based or fear based. You may think, "I am feeling competitive". Is feeling competitive a love based or a fear based emotion? It depends. You may have to stop and say, " I'm feeling I want to compete with this person. Am I afraid that I won't be able to match this person in something?" Then you are feeling fear. If you say "I'm feeling competitive because I wish to do the very best that I can. I know I have a strong body and wish to compete" then you are doing it with love.

How you define things becomes your reality. It is very tempting as human beings to judge things as good or bad, right or wrong. Things are not good or bad – things are fear or love. If you stopped seeing situations as "good or bad," and started recognizing them as "fear based or love based," the world might start making more sense.

Many people are waiting to find something that will make them feel joy - a new job, or a new love. Joy is a natural state of being for all human beings, and happiness is a state of mind. You can be happy, but not constantly happy. You can be joyful constantly. This means that the first thing that is necessary is to believe that you are joyful this moment and then say to yourself, "How can I create this job at this moment to be joyful, and then this new love to be joyful in my life?" and not, "I will need a new job and a new love and then I will be joyful." Much of our lack of joy is caused by focusing on attempting to make others joyful instead of ourselves.

The way to find a being to enjoy your life with is to first become a joyful being.

When you are making your day-to-day decisions, ask, "Will this enhance or detract from my sense of joy, and will this enhance or detract from my sense of freedom?"

It is not necessary for all to agree to choose love in order for love to become the dominant feeling. We are all connected. It spreads like a cold or flu. It is much nicer to spread, but it is a similar phenomenon.

If we were to leave you with one suggestion,
It would be that everyday you are presented
With numerous opportunities to make choices.
The greatest gift that your planet has
Is free will, emotion, and choices.
So today, as in all days, you will have a choice
To respond in a love-based or a fear based fashion.
Each time you choose to respond
And to act in a love based fashion
You are changing the world.
You are more powerful than you can ever imagine,
And we thank you for this
As you are aiding our species and all love based species.
—The Light Collective

You Are Responsible is the second most important
of the principles.
You cannot change anyone but yourself, but by
changing yourself
You change everyone because we are all one.
You could potentially be much more joyful
If you would work harder on changing yourself
And less hard on changing others.
If all beings did this,
Great change would take place.
—The Light Collective

You Are Greatly Admired & Feared By Other Beings

Principle Eight
You Are Responsible

As eternal beings, we choose our various lives; where we will live, what type of being we will be, what we will do, etc. Of this, the Light Collective says, *"Earth is not the easiest place to learn, to choose, so only brave souls choose to be human. It is known, you are known, as mavericks, adventurers, and some would say foolish. You are greatly admired and feared by most of the beings that choose quieter lifetimes in quieter cosmos."*

You come to earth for a purpose, which is to go and to learn how to be joyful in the circumstances that you have chosen. You have chosen to come into this planet at this time with members of your soul collective. You and your parents had a cup of coffee in spirit and determined who would be the father and who would be the child, and some of the circumstances that would happen - many of them fear based. You chose to enter into these circumstances for the purpose of learning not to be fearful, but learning to choose love.

All things are not predetermined. Once you are on the planet you make mistakes and you choose fear. Some came in thinking they would be a certain way, and then chose fear and became another way.

You can't always protect yourself from someone who is dangerous or criminal, but even there you can choose your response. While it may not change the action, it will change how you view the action, and your response will change everything.

The Light Collective says, "No one has pre-planned your life. Prior to entering your physical body you entered into a plan. You decided your plan for coming here. When you got here you don't remember your plan. You create your plan and your friend creates his plan, and your friend's friend creates her plan, and then you all attempt to not trip over each other's plan. On a cosmic level you all join in on a cosmic plan and on your collective plan, and somehow or other you muddle with it. There is no great God plan, for God's great plan was to allow you to plan. And God has wondered ever since!"

"You will have many purposes, minor purposes we would call them, in which you are called to become teachers and healers and other growers of beings and sellers of items and various other fine things, but your major purpose is to grow in who you already are. You do that by communicating with those who are in your community and then that will spread."

It's always your choice as to how you come to this earth. It's also a principle that many people don't find appealing, to think they are responsible for the life they are currently living, that they have chosen and created their life. That's true, however you may not have chosen all of the ways in which it played out, of course you have only control over your own life. There are many others in free will circumstances who are playing out different scenarios, and so of course this is what makes life so interesting here on earth.

There is often a question about life purpose.
All beings wish to grow,
And also to aid in some fashion on your planet and others.
We applaud your desire to do so,
And we would say that now is the time to do so.
The way to do so is to go deep within you and ask yourself
"What brings me joy?"
Then to follow that path.
If you no longer focus on what helps others
And go to what brings you joy,
By your joy you are improving the world.
We would suggest to you that even for one day if you would think,
"Today I will do only what brings me joy."
Imagine a world in which that would be a function.
—The Light Collective

You find your safety on your inside,
Your core connection with each other and the Divine.
When you make that contact with these truths:
You are one,
You are eternal,
You create your world with your thoughts
And you activate them with your emotions,
You are responsible for them,
With these truths you see
Come total safety.
—The Light Collective

Kathryn Harwig has been an intuitive since birth and started channeling the Light Collective approximately 10 years ago. She grew up on a farm in Hinckley, Minnesota, where her psychic abilities were seen by her parents and neighbors as a surprising and yet accepted skill. She went on to attend the University of St. Cloud, Minnesota, receiving a Bachelor of Science degree (magna cum laude) in Psychology and Sociology.

After graduation she became a probation officer in Minneapolis, Minnesota. For many years she supervised and wrote pre-sentence investigations regarding adult felons. She then attended the University of Minnesota in a graduate program of Criminal Justice Studies, specializing in the prediction of dangerousness. In 1982 she graduated cum laude from William Mitchell College of Law with a Doctorate in Law. She was a successful partner in a law firm for many years before leaving the practice of law to pursue her full time career as a psychic, medium, speaker and writer.

Kathryn is the author of five books, Your Life In the Palm Of Your Hand (1994), The Millennium Effect (1996), The Intuitive Advantage (2000), The Angel in the Big Pink Hat (2005), and Palm Visions (2007). Her books have also been published in German and Dutch. She is also a monthly columnist for Edge Life Magazine where she shares monthly intuitive insights with a circulation of approximately 45,000 readers.

Kathryn appears regularly on television and radio. She has been featured on the Arts & Entertainment network's "The Unexplained", and on Court TV's "Psychic Detectives." She is a regular monthly guest on the Eleanor Mondale and Susie Jones radio show on WCCO AM in Minneapolis, Minnesota.

Kathryn has trained thousands of people to use their intuition to maximize their career goals, relationships, and life skills. Her monthly intuitive forums are attended by hundreds of people who gather to hear her guides, the Light Collective, share their wisdom.

Kathryn calls herself a professional wanderer. She has traveled to over 90 countries and been featured on radio and television in Jamaica, Brazil, Australia, Holland and Germany.

About The Author

Dorothy is the loving mother of three wonderful grown children, Paul, Laura, and Lisa, and the grandmother of seven awesome grandchildren, Victoria, Matthew, Ricky, Mason, Andy, Dylan, and one on the way! She lives in St. Michael, Minnesota a small community near Minneapolis. When she is not busy reading, traveling, and playing with her grandchildren, she finds time to continue her life long passion of sharing knowledge that will assist others in living fulfilling lives.

Although Dorothy grew up in a typical middle class family in the Midwest in the fifties and sixties, she was aware that life is often difficult. As the Light Collective says:
"Joy is your legacy. You came to this earth knowing in fact that it was a difficult place to find joy. You came to this difficult place because that was the purpose, to come to a difficult place and then learn to find joy."

Her quest for the keys to a joyous life began in college, where she earned degrees in Early Childhood Education, Special Education, Psychology, and Counseling. Now retired, she taught and coordinated programs in the Minneapolis Public Schools for 35 fascinating years.

When Dorothy discovered the Light Collective's teachings, she realized they are what she had been looking for her entire life: a foundation and guide for a life of joy, freedom, and abundance. Their teachings are not new, and yet many (including Dorothy until recently) have not heard of them.

The Eight Principles to Inner Peace and *Invest In Joy: Teachings of the*

Light Collective, upon which this book is based, are the beginning of Dorothy's new teaching career. She shares this knowledge with others, so they too can benefit, as she has, from the wisdom, and feelings of peace and empowerment the teachings bring.

Contact Dorothy Lee at:
www.dorothylee@me.com
or
Dorothy Lee
P.O. Box 373
St. Michael, MN 55376

MORE FROM THE LIGHT COLLECTIVE

We hope you enjoyed this Light collective book.

To order

Invest In Joy
A Journey to Inner Peace and Personal Empowerment,
or
The Eight Principles To Inner Peace,
A Spiritual Guidebook to a Joyous, Free & Abundant Life

Visit my website:
www.dorothylee.us

If you would like to receive free monthly updates and advice from the Light Collective during these challenging times, as well as more helpful and fascinating information about God, mankind, and the cosmos, go to: www.dorothylee.us.

The Light Collective tells us our society is in the process of amazing change. To learn about this change and how to successfully transition to a new way of life, receive your free copy of "Change: a More Equal, Loving, and Peaceful Society," a presentation given by the Light Collective at The Minneapolis Convention Center Edge Life Expo November 2009 at: www.dorothylee.us/change

Notes

Notes

Notes

Notes

Lightning Source UK Ltd.
Milton Keynes UK
UKOW06f1653260615

254179UK00001B/146/P